I LOVE TO FISH

(Cobia Campfire)

By Joseph A. Brandenburg, III
Illustrated by Ellen Jones

Edited with love by his Grandmother,
Susan D. Brandenburg

Hi, my name is Joseph.

I'm 12 years old and I love to fish.

My dad, Joel Brandenburg,
is a charter boat captain and

I'm his first mate.

He named his fishing company after
my mom's nickname,

Ana Banana.

Today, my dad and I went on a charter.

We left at dawn,

tiptoeing out to the truck

while mom,

my little sister,

Brooke,

and our Teacup Chihuahua,

Gizmo,

were fast asleep.

We met our clients at

Little Harbor Resort,

where my dad charters

and keeps his guide boat.

The sun was sparkling on the water as we

headed out for a day of fishing!

My dad is the best captain in Apollo Beach.
He always knows where the fish are! We caught
15 **Snook**, 3 **Redfish**, 20 **Sea Trout** and 1 **Tarpon**.

After we dropped off our clients, I noticed we still had some Bait left. We had about three dozen Shrimp and about 100 **Greenbacks**.

"Dad, we've got bait left. Can we fish some more?"

"Nope.

We have to clean the boat for tomorrow's charter".

"Please, Dad!

I'll clean up the boat by myself!"

"Okay, son,

but you'll have to clean it up as soon as we get back.

Let's see if we can find some **Cobia**".

Cobia is my favorite fish – to catch and to eat.

They are big, brown fish that live near any structure.

They are also called Lemon Fish and Ling,

but my favorite nickname for them is Brown Bombers,

because of their color and fighting ability.

We zigzag through **buoys** looking for Cobia

daisy-chaining (circling)

on the surface around the buoys.

We go by ten buoys and nothing.
Then, at the very next buoy,
there is a nice-sized
Cobia.

I put a shrimp on my hook and cast it right in front of his face on the surface of the water. He sucks it in with a sound like someone slurping spaghetti. That sound is music to my ears. It tells me the fight is on!

He knows he's hooked,
so he heads towards the buoy where he can wrap the line against
the **buoy chain** and snap it.

I have learned how to direct him the other way.

Luke 5:1-11

We get him in open water and he races away.
Dad's up in the **tower** chasing him with
the boat while I am down
below reeling him in.

I can feel my Cobia
getting tired.
As a last attempt
at freedom,
he **digs down** as deep
as he can go,
but I **pump** him up
by reeling down
and pulling up
again and again.

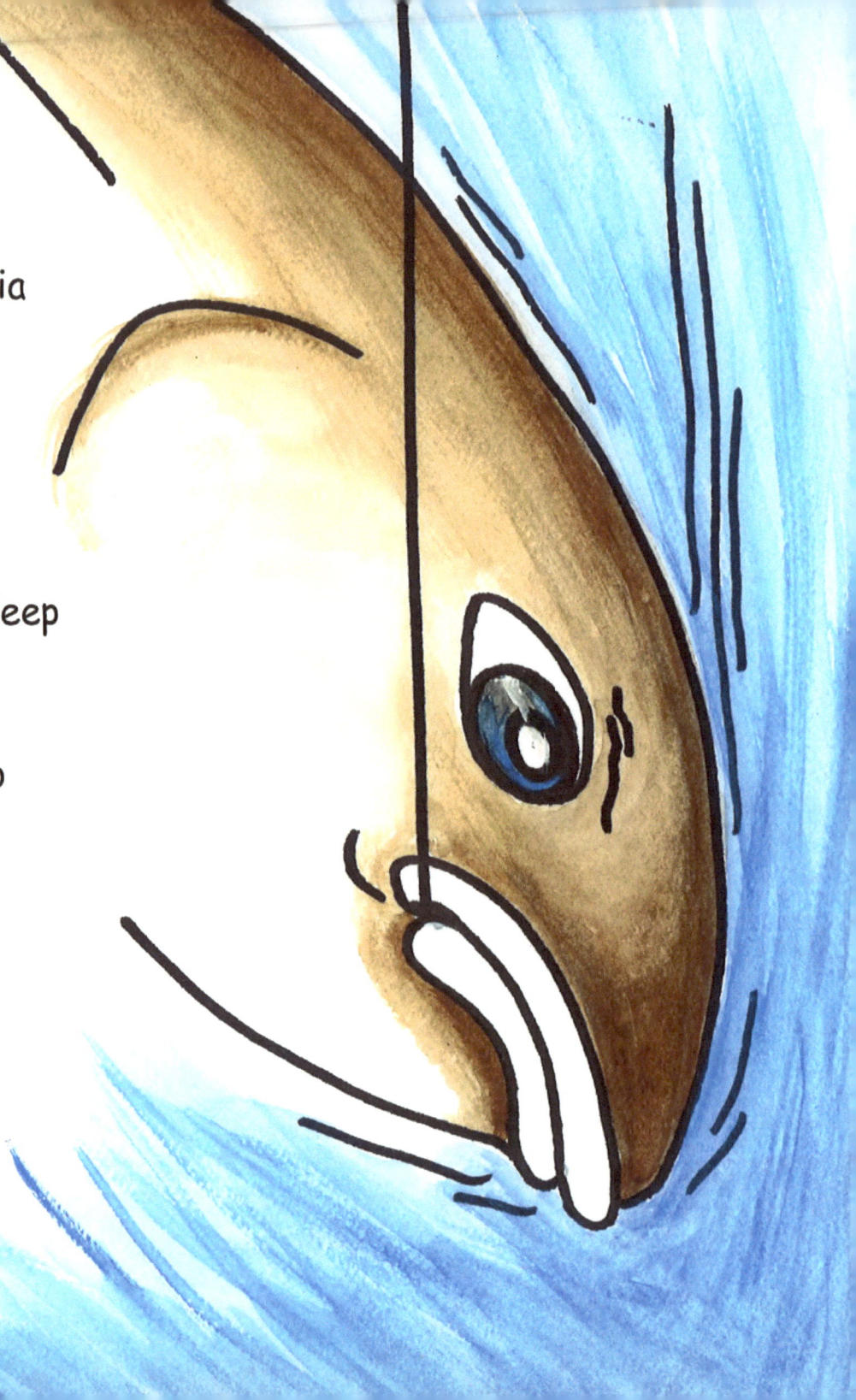

My dad knows the Cobia is almost ready to come in the boat,

so he gets down from the tower and grabs

the **gaff**.

We get him in the boat and put him in the

cooler as fast as possible.

As we pull up to the dock,

my sister Brooke is waiting,

with our little dog Gizmo at her feet.

"Joseph, what did you catch?" yells Brooke.

I hold up a 45-inch, 30 pound Cobia.

Brooke's eyes get huge. She says,

"We're going to have a party tonight!"

"Joseph,
    you're cleaning up the boat,
                    right?"

my dad reminds me.

"Yes sir!"

(Ahhh man! That's the only part of fishing I don't love!)

I get the hose, a scrub brush, a bucket of bleach, and
go to work. I know I have to do this right the first
time, or I'll have to do it all over and miss the party.

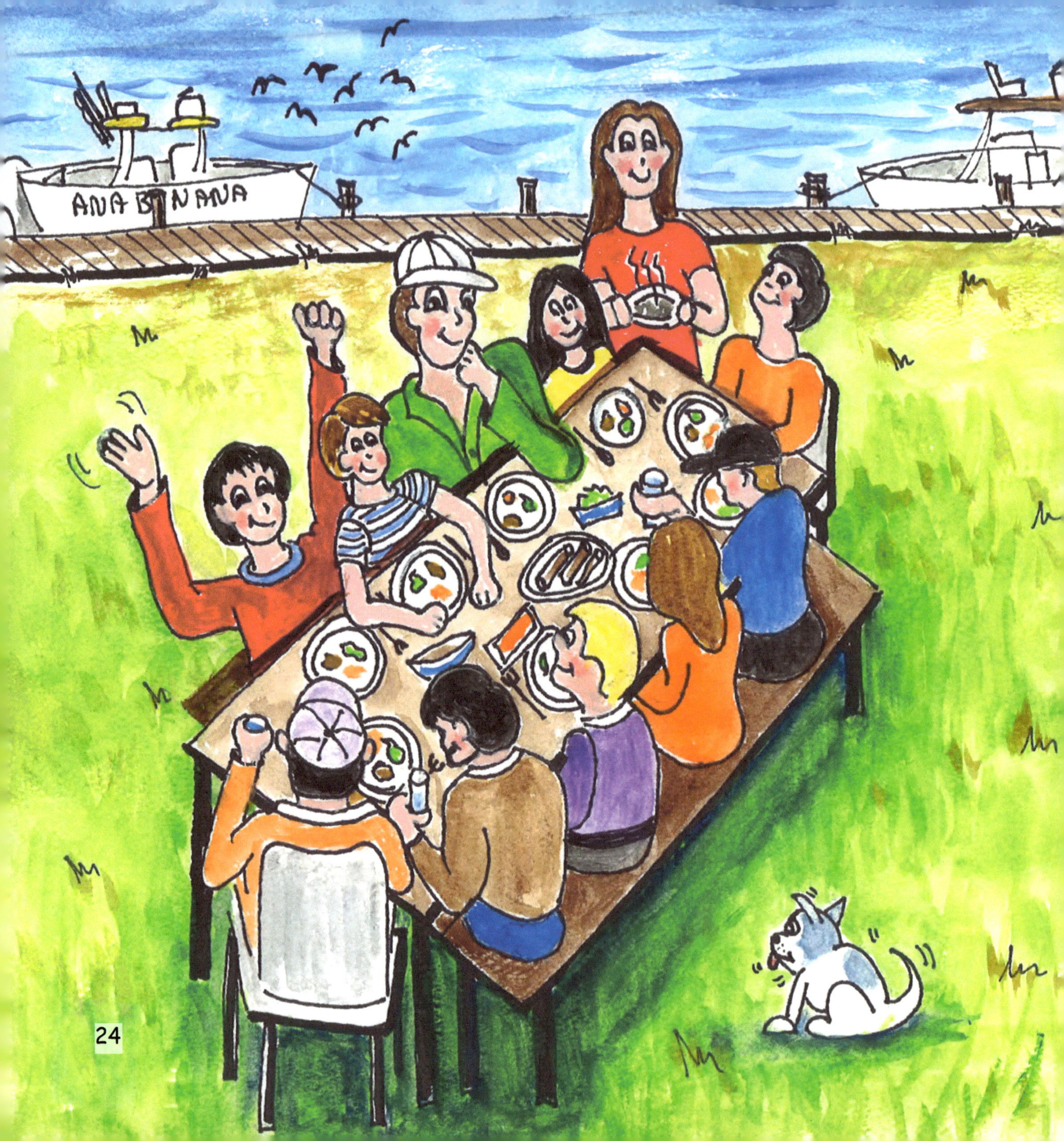
ANA B NANA

Dad **filets** the fish.

Mom fries it with **Everglades Seasoning**™

while Brooke goes to invite some

neighbors over for a

Cobia party

with corn, **hushpuppies**,

and my mom's favorite - black beans and rice.

After we eat,

we play a game of backyard football.

We all join in until it gets too dark and then we sit around the campfire and tell fish stories.

Today, everyone agrees that

my fish story

is the best one of all!

Glossary

Snook – A tropical fish with a black stripe down the middle and an elongated lower jaw.

Redfish – A red fish found mainly in Southern waters of the U.S.A.

Sea Trout – A short fish with dark green topside, black spots and a silvery bottom –found in waters around the world.

Tarpon – A large silvery fish – one of the most sought-after trophy game fish in the world.

Shrimp – Shellfish, sometimes used for bait (everything, including humans, will eat shrimp).

Greenbacks – A small bait fish with a green back.

Cobia – A large tropical fish also known as a Lemon Fish and a Ling.

Buoy – A navigation marker floating in the water to help guide watercraft.

Daisy-Chaining – A fisherman's term for circling.

Buoy Chain – Attached to an anchor so the buoy stays in the same place.

Tower – A high structure in the middle of the boat where you can drive and see fish better.

Gaff – A long, sturdy hook designed to pull large fish into the boat.

Pump – A technique used by fishermen to reel in big fish.

Dig – Dive down.

Filet – A way to butcher fish.

Everglades Seasoning™ – A great seasoning that makes fish taste better.

Hushpuppies – A dough ball made with onions and deep-fried.

Little Harbor Resort – An exclusive Florida resort –
www.staylittleharbor.com

www.ingramcontent.com/pod-product-compliance
Lightning Source LLC
Chambersburg PA
CBHW041239040426
42445CB00004B/81